A DAY IN THE LIFE OF A
Theater Set Designer

by Ann Hodgman
Photography by Gayle Jann

Troll Associates

Library of Congress Cataloging in Publication Data

Hodgman, Ann.
    A day in the life of a theater set designer.

    Summary: Follows a set designer through her day as she
works on creating sets for plays, movies, and
television shows.
       1. Conaway-Parsloe, Linda—Juvenile literature.
2. Set designers—United States—Biography—Juvenile
literature. [1. Set designers. 2. Conaway-Parsloe,
Linda. 3. Occupations] I. Jann, Gayle, ill. II. Title.
PN2096.C66H6   1988   792'.025'0924   [B]   87-10951
ISBN 0-8167-1127-5 (lib. bdg.)
ISBN 0-8167-1128-3 (pbk.)

10 9 8 7 6 5 4 3 2 1

The author and publisher wish to thank Linda Conaway-Parsloe, Bob Paolitto,
John Romeo, Pat Woodbridge, Candice Dunn, Joanne Hanley and Donald Al-
brecht of the Museum of the Moving Image, Arnold Abramson, Neil Bittner,
Gary Cinkead, and Marie Le Doux for their help and cooperation.

Linda Conaway begins her workday with some research in her design studio at home. As a set designer and art director, she creates sets for plays, movies, and television shows. Linda must be well-informed on a variety of subjects. Today she is studying nineteenth-century architecture, clothing and furniture for a historical play.

Next, Linda sets up her day's appointments. She works both at her home in the suburbs and at a second design studio she has in New York. Each day may involve meetings in both places. Because she spends so much time traveling, and meets with so many different people, Linda has learned to be extremely well organized.

Linda sits down at her drafting board to review some work. She recently designed a sportscasters' set for a cable TV network, and the set is now being installed. She will be visiting the TV studio later in the day to make sure there are no problems. Her job as a set designer demands many different skills, from engineering to budgeting.

Seen from above, the set has five sides. It includes seating for four people, several TV monitors, and graphics. Linda is always careful to present ideas and drawings for her designs in a professional manner. She knows that many people will be looking at her designs, both before she is hired and while each set is being built.

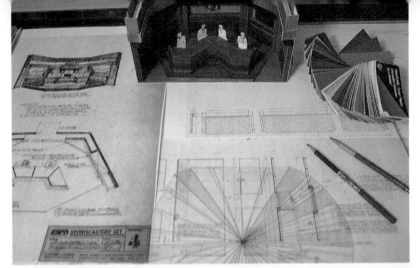

When Linda met with the TV show's producers and directors, she showed them detailed plans for the set she had designed. She also brought along samples of materials to be used, as well as a color selector for choosing the exact colors the set would be painted. Later, a scale model of her final design was built.

Not all of Linda's designs are as streamlined and modern-looking as the sportscasters' set. Her portfolio is filled with photographs and drawings of other work she has done. For a children's opera called "Two Fiddlers," she designed a timeless theater set that conveys a feeling of enchantment and wonder.

By mid-morning, Linda is busy running errands. First, she picks up some work a local copy shop has done for her. Then she stops off at a graphics shop. There, she examines some film of her design for a title sequence for a TV show. Linda retouches one negative herself, using thick red paint, which will not show in the photo.

One of Linda's other projects is designing props for a movie. She must create special newspapers, with headlines and photos to match stories provided by the movie's scriptwriters. Since the movie is set in the 1930s, the newspapers must look old-fashioned. In a typesetter's shop, Linda chooses a typeface that will look authentic.

Linda's final errand is a visit to a local blueprinting shop, where copies of prints for yet another project will be made. Linda will give the copies to the show's director, producer, and lighting designer, and to the people who will actually build and paint the set.

After her errands, Linda drives to the city. Her first stop is at a museum in a movie studio, where a special display shows some of the props Linda created for the movie *The Cotton Club*. Linda worked on the film for seven months, designing everything from storefronts to matchbox covers.

Linda gives the museum's curator a poster she designed for a new film. Then she visits a special exhibit of old movie cameras and projectors. On her way out she checks her appointment book. She does not have to be at the cable TV studio until late in the afternoon. This means she has time to make several other stops first.

In her design studio in the city, Linda revises a few computer files. Like many set designers, she finds a computer helpful for organizing each new job. For example, one television show she worked on had twelve sets. With the computer, Linda was able to organize easily the huge list of furniture and props needed for each set.

Often Linda finds that talking to other artists and observing their work helps her with her own designs. After leaving her studio, she visits an artist she met through a local organization for artists and designers. She hopes that studying some of his work will give her an inspiration for a theater set she is planning.

Next, Linda stops by a film studio's art department. She wants to check on a poster she designed for another film. Linda worked on the film for two months and was responsible for all the graphic arts work for the set.

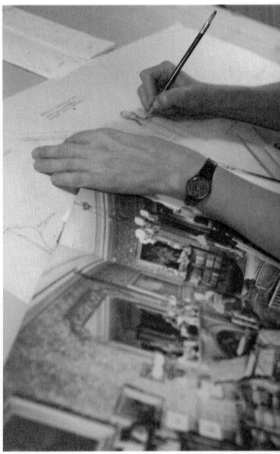

An assistant art director on the film adds some details to a movie set that will be built in the scenery shop. These drawings will be used to figure out material orders, schedules, and labor needs. They will be referred to again and again during the actual construction of the set.

An important part of Linda's job is keeping up with developments in theater sets. She stops in to visit a scenic artists' shop that is well known for its stage backdrops. The owner shows Linda the designer's painting of the set. This is called a "paint elevation." The backdrop has been made using the paint elevation as a guide.

Workers glue muslin pieces onto a "scrim," or transparent backdrop, for a Broadway show. The scrim creates a special effect often used by set designers. The painted muslin is too thick to see through. When the backdrop is in place on stage, the muslin sections will appear to float in midair.

Even though this backdrop will be placed toward the rear of the stage, its details are painted very carefully. Dozens of brushes are required to create the right effect, and the shop keeps them carefully organized. Large quantities of painting supplies are kept in stock at all times.

Linda has also worked on designs for soap opera sets. A friend has asked her to stop by the set of a daytime soap opera. She wants Linda's advice on a lighting effect that will create the shape of a window on a wall of the set. Linda reviews the lighting plans for the room, and makes a few suggestions.

The average TV soap opera has about twenty sets. Usually only a few of them are kept up permanently. The rest must be changed and redressed every day. The art director and the assistants must keep organized files of all sets and decoration. The needed daily changes must be done quickly and efficiently.

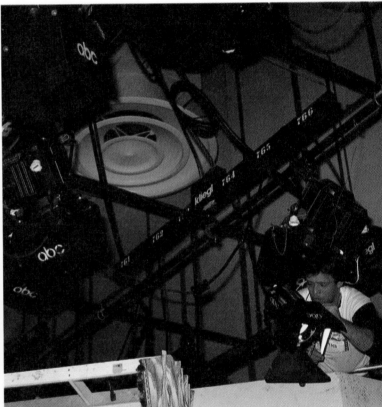

A lighting technician uses a long pole to focus one of the lamps used on the set. Nearby, another technician adjusts the "barn doors" on a lamp, to direct its beam more precisely. Each lamp is numbered, and is attached by a cable to a large dimmer panel. The dimmer panel controls the intensity of all the lights.

In the control room, the lighting designer studies the set. Before the taping, the director and lighting designer watch a quick run-through of each scene. Three different cameras, each with its own monitor, are used. The director uses a headset to supervise the camera technicians, then chooses the images that will be seen by the viewers.

It's time for Linda to go to the cable TV studio where her sportscasters' set is being installed. A few days ago, she took care of the final details at the scenery shop. She examined all of the elements of the set, from the sportscasters' console to the sliding panels behind it. She also chose the stain that would be used on the console and paneling.

Now the finished set has been almost completely assembled at the cable TV studio. Linda wants to be there to watch the installation of the final pieces and to oversee the finishing touches. Construction workers measure the set for the carpet that will be glued to the walls.

Next, a strong carpet adhesive is applied to the walls. Carpet is used for several reasons. It is non-reflective, so there will be no glare or harsh shadows when lights are aimed at the set. It has a more interesting texture than paint, and it will also give the set a softer look.

It takes several workers to handle the large sections of carpet and position them correctly. Linda has already checked the carpet against the sample swatches to make sure the correct color was delivered. The medium gray color will provide a neutral background with no distractions, so the sportscasters will be the focal point on the set.

Workers install the "logo"—the cable network's symbol—above the opening in each wall on the set. Lights from behind the plexiglass "light box" will illuminate the logo. Since it is the network's main identification, its placement is very important.

As workers continue assembling the announcers' desks, Linda examines the entire set. When designing sets, she must specify what materials and paint will be used. If the sets contain lights, she must also indicate where the ventilation openings will be, and where the electric cables will be connected.

In the studio's control room, a technician shows
Linda how the set will look on a television screen.
This gives her a chance to check minor details, like
the intensity of the lights. A televised set looks so
different from one seen close up that Linda must
check the monitors again and again.

At the end of her long day, Linda stops off at a local health club. She enjoys working out, and regular exercise sessions help her to keep in shape. Linda also enjoys the busy pace of her job and the challenges she faces as a set designer. Each new project is another opportunity for her to use her designing skills in a new and exciting way.